# MOTO-X FREE STYLE

BY JACK DAVID

TORQUE
™

BELLWETHER MEDIA • MINNEAPOLIS, MN

Are you ready to take it to the extreme?
Torque books thrust you into the action-packed world
of sports, vehicles, and adventure. These books may
include dirt, smoke, fire, and dangerous stunts.
WARNING: read at your own risk.

This edition first published in 2008 by Bellwether Media.

No part of this publication may be reproduced in whole or in part without written permission of the publisher. For information regarding permission, write to Bellwether Media Inc., Attention: Permissions Department, Post Office Box 1C, Minnetonka, MN 55345-9998.

Library of Congress Cataloging-in-Publication Data
David, Jack, 1968-
  Moto-x freestyle / by Jack David.
    p. cm. -- (Torque. Action sports)
  Summary: "Photographs of amazing feats accompany engaging information about moto-X freestyle. The combination of high-interest subject matter and light text is intended to engage readers in grades 3 through 7"--Provided by publisher.
  Includes bibliographical references and index.
  ISBN-13: 978-1-60014-125-6 (hardcover : alk. paper)
  ISBN-10: 1-60014-125-0 (hardcover : alk. paper)
  1. Motocross--Juvenile literature. I. Title.

GV1060.12.D38 2008
796.7'56--dc22                                              2007016793

# CONTENTS

# THE EXCITEMENT OF MOTO-X FREESTYLE

The engine of a Moto-X Freestyle bike hums. The rider leans forward as the bike speeds toward a huge dirt ramp. It is the last jump in the competition.

The dirt bike races up the ramp. It launches high into the air. The rider places his feet below the handlebars and stands up. He raises his arms as he sails through the air. Then he slides back onto the bike and makes a perfect landing. The crowd roars. The rider has landed a **cliffhanger**.

# WHAT IS MOTO-X FREESTYLE?

Moto-X Freestyle or "FMX" is one of the world's most thrilling motor sports. Riders jump their bikes off of huge ramps. They launch into the air and do dangerous tricks.

Motocross freestyle grew out of **motocross racing**. Racers liked to do tricks when they went over dirt jumps. They did simple tricks such as **no-handers** to pump up the crowd. The tricks became popular and led to the new sport of freestyle.

Freestyle motocross bikes are **modified** to stand up to the rough treatment of crashes and big jumps. They're made as lightweight as possible. They have strong springs and shock absorbers to soften big landings.

Most freestyle bikes also include various handles on the body. Riders grab onto these handles to perform many of their tricks. Freestyle motocross riders also use very small seats. This gives them a better range of motion for performing tricks.

Safety is a big concern for riders. Missing a big trick can be dangerous. Riders wear helmets, goggles, gloves, and other protective clothing. Many riders also wear elbow and knee pads for extra protection.

# MOTO-X FREESTYLE
# IN ACTION

Riders in standard freestyle motocross competitions do rehearsed routines. Riders have from 90 seconds to several minutes to land as many tricks as possible. Judges score the routines based on the quality and variety of tricks. The highest possible score is 100.

Best trick events are also thrilling. Each rider gets three tries at the same trick. Only the best score counts. The backflip is a popular trick. The **Superman** is also common. Riders stretch their bodies out over the bike without holding the handlebars. They look like Superman flying through the air!

Riders are constantly inventing new tricks. Their creativity helps make freestyle motocross such a heart-pounding extreme sport.

# GLOSSARY

**cliffhanger**—an FMX trick in which a rider stands on or under the handlebars while in the air

**modify**—to change; motocross racing bikes are modified for motocross freestyle.

**motocross racing**—a sport in which riders drive dirt bikes around a small dirt course; motocross tracks include sharp turns and huge jumps.

**no-hander**—a simple trick where riders raise their hands off of the handlebars

**Superman**—a trick in which riders stretch their bodies out over the bike without touching it

# TO LEARN MORE

## AT THE LIBRARY

David, Jack. *Motocross Racing*.
Minneapolis, Minn.: Bellwether Media, 2008.

Doeden, Matt. *Motocross Freestyle*.
Mankato, Minn.: Capstone Press, 2005.

Levy, Janey. *Freestyle Motocross*.
New York: PowerKids Press, 2007.

## ON THE WEB

Learning more about moto-x
freestyle is as easy as 1, 2, 3.

1. Go to www.factsurfer.com
2. Enter "moto-x freestyle" into search box.
3. Click the "Surf" button and you will see a list
   of related web sites.

With factsurfer.com, finding more
information is just a click away.

# INDEX

The photographs in this book are provided courtesy of: Stephen Coburn, front cover; Tony Donaldson/Shazamm/ESPN Images, p. 3; Bakke/Shazamm/ESPN Images, pp. 4-5, 20; Markus Paulsen, p. 7; Shazamm/ESPN Images, pp. 8, 9, 10, 11, 13; Bakke/Shazamm/ESPN Images, p. 18; Dom Cooley, p. 19; Tomas Zuccareno, p. 21.